Influence and Persuasion

HBR Emotional Intelligence Series

How to be human at work

The HBR Emotional Intelligence Series features smart, essential reading on the human side of professional life from the pages of *Harvard Business Review*.

Authentic Leadership

Empathy

Happiness

Influence and Persuasion

Mindfulness

Resilience

Other books on emotional intelligence from *Harvard Business Review*:

HBR's 10 Must Reads on Emotional Intelligence

HBR Guide to Emotional Intelligence

Influence and Persuasion

HBR EMOTIONAL INTELLIGENCE SERIES

Harvard Business Review Press

Boston, Massachusetts

Library of Congress cataloging information is forthcoming

ISBN 978-1-63369-393-7
eISBN 978-1-63369-394-4

The paper used in this publication meets the requirements of the American National Standard for Permanence of Paper for Publications and Documents in Libraries and Archives Z39.48-1992.

Contents

Contents

Influence and Persuasion

HBR EMOTIONAL INTELLIGENCE SERIES

1

Understand the Four Components of Influence

By Nick Morgan

We've all encountered people who say less but what they say matters more; people who know how to use silence to dominate an exchange. So having influence means more than just doing all the talking; it's about taking charge and understanding the roles that positional power, emotion, expertise, and nonverbal signals play. These four aspects of influence are essential to master if you want to succeed as a leader.

Take *positional power*. If you have it, influence becomes a relatively simple proposition. People with power over others tend to talk more, to interrupt more, and to guide the conversation more, by picking the topics, for example.

If you don't have the positional power in a particular situation, then, expect to talk less, interrupt less, and choose the topics of conversation less. After all, exercising their right to talk more about the subjects they care for is one of the ways that people with positional power demonstrate it.

What do you do if you want to challenge the positional authority? Perhaps you have a product, or an idea, or a company you want to sell, and you have the ear of someone who can buy it. How do you get control in that kind of situation?

The second aspect of influence is *emotion*, and using it is one way to counteract positional power and generally to dominate a conversation. When the other side has the power and you have the emotion, something closer to parity is possible. Indeed, passion can sweep away authority, when it's well supported and the speaker is well prepared. We've all witnessed that happen when a young unknown performer disarms and woos the judges, devastating the competition, in one of those talent competitions. The purity and power of the emotion in the performance is enough to silence—and enlist—the judges despite their positional authority. Indeed, the impassioned speech, the plea for clemency, the summation to the jury that brings them to tears and wins the case for the defendant—this is the stuff of Hollywood climaxes.

Passion often links with *expertise*, the third aspect of influence. And indeed, you can dominate the conversation, beating out positional power, if you have both passion and expertise. The diffident expert's voice is sometimes lost in the clamor of people wanting to be heard. So expertise without passion is not always effective, but if it's patient, it can be the last person standing in a debate and thereby get its turn.

The final aspect of influence is the subtlest of the four and as such rarely can trump either positional authority or passion. But in rare instances, artfully manipulated, I have seen it prevail. What is it? It is the mastery of the dance of human interaction.

We have very little conscious awareness of this aspect of influence, but we are all participants in it with more or less expertise. We learn at a very early age that conversation is a pas de deux, a game that two (or more) people play that involves breathing, winking, nodding, eye contact, head tilts, hand gestures, and a whole series of subtle nonverbal signals that help both parties communicate with each other.

Indeed, conversation is much less functional without these *nonverbal signals*. That's why phone conversations are nowhere near as satisfying as in-person encounters and why conference calls inevitably involve lots more interruptions, miscues, and cross talking. We're not getting the signals we're used to getting to help us know when the other person is ready to hand the conversational baton on to us, and vice versa.

Can you manage influence only using this fourth aspect? I have seen it done in certain situations, but the other three aspects will usually trump this one. Nonetheless, I once watched a senior executive effortlessly dominate a roomful of people who were ostensibly equal—a group of researchers gathered from around the world to discuss the future of IT. Within a few minutes, everyone in the room was unconsciously deferring to this executive, even though he had no positional power and was not particularly passionate about the subject. His mastery of the subtle signals of conversational cuing was profound, and soon he had everyone dancing to his verbal beat. It was beautiful to watch; he showed complete conversational mastery in action.

Influence, then, is a measure of how much skin the participants have in the game, and most of us are unconscious experts at measuring it. To wield it, you need to have the edge in at least one of its four aspects—and preferably more than one.

NICK MORGAN is an author, speaker, coach, and the president and founder of Public Words, a communications consulting firm.

Excerpted from the author's book *Power Cues: The Subtle Science of Leading Groups, Persuading Others, and Maximizing Your Personal Impact* (product #11710), Harvard Business Review Press, 2014.

2

Harnessing the Science of Persuasion

By Robert Cialdini

A lucky few have it; most of us do not. A handful of gifted "naturals" simply know how to capture an audience, sway the undecided, and convert the opposition. Watching these masters of persuasion work their magic is at once impressive and frustrating. What's impressive is not just the easy way they use charisma and eloquence to convince others to do as they ask. It's also how eager those others are to do what's requested of them, as if the persuasion itself were a favor they couldn't wait to repay.

The frustrating part of the experience is that these born persuaders are often unable to account for their remarkable skill or pass it on to others. Their way with people is an art, and artists as a rule are far better at doing than at explaining. Most of them can't offer much help to those of us who possess no more than the ordinary quotient of charisma and eloquence but who still have to wrestle with leadership's fundamental challenge: getting things done through others. That challenge is painfully familiar to corporate executives, who every day have to figure out how to motivate and direct a highly individualistic work force. Playing the "Because I'm the boss" card is out. Even if it weren't demeaning and demoralizing for all concerned, it would be out of place in a world where cross-functional teams, joint ventures, and intercompany partnerships have blurred the lines of authority. In such an environment, persuasion skills exert far greater influence over others' behavior than formal power structures do.

Which brings us back to where we started. Persuasion skills may be more necessary than ever, but how can executives acquire them if the most talented practitioners can't pass them along? By looking to science. For the past five decades, behavioral scientists have conducted experiments that shed considerable light on the way certain interactions lead people to concede, comply, or change. This research shows that persuasion works by appealing to a limited set of deeply rooted human drives and needs, and it does so in predictable ways. Persuasion, in other words, is governed by basic principles that can be taught, learned, and applied. By mastering these principles, executives can bring scientific rigor to the business of securing consensus, cutting deals, and winning concessions. In the pages that follow, I describe six fundamental principles of persuasion and suggest a few ways that executives can apply them in their own organizations.

The principle of liking:
People like those who like them.

*The application: Uncover real similarities
and offer genuine praise.*

The retailing phenomenon known as the Tupperware party is a vivid illustration of this principle in action. The demonstration party for Tupperware products is hosted by an individual, almost always a woman, who invites to her home an array of friends, neighbors, and relatives. The guests' affection for their hostess predisposes them to buy from her, a dynamic that was confirmed by a 1990 study of purchase decisions made at demonstration parties. The researchers, Jonathan Frenzen and Harry Davis, writing in the *Journal of Consumer Research*, found that the guests' fondness for their hostess weighed twice as heavily in their purchase decisions as their regard for the products they bought. So when guests at a Tupperware party buy something, they aren't just buying to please themselves. They're buying to please their hostess as well.

What's true at Tupperware parties is true for business in general: If you want to influence people, win friends. How? Controlled research has identified several factors that reliably increase liking, but two stand out as especially compelling—similarity and praise. Similarity literally draws people together. In one experiment, reported in a 1968 article in the *Journal of Personality*, participants stood physically closer to one another after learning that they shared political beliefs and social values. And in a 1963 article in *American Behavioral Scientists*, researcher F. B. Evans used demographic data from insurance company records to demonstrate that prospects were more willing to purchase a policy from a salesperson who was akin to them in age, religion, politics, or even cigarette-smoking habits.

Managers can use similarities to create bonds with a recent hire, the head of another department, or even a new boss. Informal conversations during the workday create an ideal opportunity to discover at least one common area of enjoyment, be it a hobby, a college basketball team, or reruns of *Seinfeld*. The important thing is to establish the bond early because it creates a presumption of goodwill and trustworthiness in every subsequent encounter. It's much easier to build support for a new project when the people you're trying to persuade are already inclined in your favor.

Praise, the other reliable generator of affection, both charms and disarms. Sometimes the praise doesn't even have to be merited. Researchers at the University of North Carolina writing in the *Journal of Experimental Social Psychology* found that men felt the greatest regard for an individual who flattered them unstintingly even if the comments were untrue. And in their book *Interpersonal Attraction* (Addison-Wesley, 1978), Ellen Berscheid and Elaine

Hatfield Walster presented experimental data showing that positive remarks about another person's
traits, attitude, or performance reliably generates liking in return, as well as willing compliance with the
wishes of the person offering the praise.

Along with cultivating a fruitful relationship, adroit
managers can also use praise to repair one that's dam-
aged or unproductive. Imagine you're the manager of
a good-sized unit within your organization. Your work
frequently brings you into contact with another manager—call him Dan—whom you have come to dislike.
No matter how much you do for him, it's not enough.
Worse, he never seems to believe that you're doing the
best you can for him. Resenting his attitude and his
obvious lack of trust in your abilities and in your good
faith, you don't spend as much time with him as you
know you should; in consequence, the performance of
both his unit and yours is deteriorating.

The research on praise points toward a strategy
for fixing the relationship. It may be hard to find, but

there has to be something about Dan you can sincerely admire, whether it's his concern for the people in his department, his devotion to his family, or simply his work ethic. In your next encounter with him, make an appreciative comment about that trait. Make it clear that in this case at least, you value what he values. I predict that Dan will relax his relentless negativity and give you an opening to convince him of your competence and good intentions.

The principle of reciprocity: People repay in kind.

The application: Give what you want to receive.

Praise is likely to have a warming and softening effect on Dan because, ornery as he is, he is still human and subject to the universal human tendency to treat people the way they treat him. If you have ever caught yourself smiling at a coworker just because he or she smiled first, you know how this principle works.

Charities rely on reciprocity to help them raise funds. For years, for instance, the Disabled American Veterans organization, using only a well-crafted fund-raising letter, garnered a very respectable 18% rate of response to its appeals. But when the group started enclosing a small gift in the envelope, the response rate nearly doubled to 35%. The gift—personalized address labels—was extremely modest, but it wasn't what prospective donors received that made the difference. It was that they had gotten anything at all.

What works in that letter works at the office, too. It's more than an effusion of seasonal spirit, of course, that impels suppliers to shower gifts on purchasing departments at holiday time. In 1996, purchasing managers admitted to an interviewer from *Inc.* magazine that after having accepted a gift from a supplier, they were willing to purchase products and services they would have otherwise declined. Gifts also have a startling effect on retention. I have encouraged readers of my book to send me examples of the principles of influence at work in their own lives. One reader, an employee of the State of Oregon, sent a letter in which she offered these reasons for her commitment to her supervisor:

He gives me and my son gifts for Christmas and gives me presents on my birthday. There is no promotion for the type of job I have, and my only choice for one is to move to another department. But I find myself resisting trying to move. My boss is reaching retirement age, and I am thinking I will be able to move out after he retires . . . [F]or now, I feel obligated to stay since he has been so nice to me.

Ultimately, though, gift giving is one of the cruder applications of the rule of reciprocity. In its more sophisticated uses, it confers a genuine first-mover advantage on any manager who is trying to foster positive attitudes and productive personal relationships in the office: Managers can elicit the desired behavior from coworkers and employees by displaying it first. Whether it's a sense of trust, a spirit of cooperation, or a pleasant demeanor, leaders should model the behavior they want to see from others.

The same holds true for managers faced with issues of information delivery and resource allocation. If you lend a member of your staff to a colleague who is shorthanded and staring at a fast-approaching deadline, you will significantly increase your chances of getting help when you need it. Your odds will improve even more if you say, when your colleague thanks you for the assistance, something like, "Sure, glad to help. I know how important it is for me to count on your help when I need it."

The principle of social proof:
People follow the lead of similar others.

The application: Use peer power
whenever it's available.

Social creatures that they are, human beings rely heavily on the people around them for cues on how to think, feel, and act. We know this intuitively, but intuition has also been confirmed by experiments, such as the one first described in 1982 in the *Journal of Applied Psychology*. A group of researchers went door-to-door in Columbia, South Carolina, soliciting donations for a charity campaign and displaying a list of neighborhood residents who had already donated to the cause. The researchers found that the longer the donor list was, the more likely those solicited would be to donate as well.

To the people being solicited, the friends' and neighbors' names on the list were a form of social evidence about how they should respond. But the evidence would not have been nearly as compelling had the names been those of random strangers. In an experiment from the 1960s, first described in the *Journal of Personality and Social Psychology*, residents of New York City were asked to return a lost wallet to its owner. They were highly likely to attempt to return the wallet when they learned that another New Yorker had previously attempted to do so. But learning that someone from a foreign country had tried to return the wallet didn't sway their decision one way or the other.

The lesson for executives from these two experiments is that persuasion can be extremely effective when it comes from peers. The science supports what most sales professionals already know: Testimonials from satisfied customers work best when the satisfied customer and the prospective customer share similar circumstances. That lesson can help a manager faced with the task of selling a new corporate initiative.

Imagine that you're trying to streamline your department's work processes. A group of veteran employees is resisting. Rather than try to convince the employees of the move's merits yourself, ask an old-timer who supports the initiative to speak up for it at a team meeting. The compatriot's testimony stands a much better chance of convincing the group than yet another speech from the boss. Stated simply, influence is often best exerted horizontally rather than vertically.

The principle of consistency: People align with their clear commitments.

The application: Make their commitments active, public, and voluntary.

Liking is a powerful force, but the work of persuasion involves more than simply making people feel warmly toward you, your idea, or your product. People need not only to like you but to feel committed to what you want them to do. Good turns are one reliable way to make people feel obligated to you. Another is to win a public commitment from them.

My own research has demonstrated that most people, once they take a stand or go on record in favor of a position, prefer to stick to it. Other studies reinforce that finding and go on to show how even a small, seemingly trivial commitment can have a powerful effect on future actions. Israeli researchers writing in 1983 in the *Personality and Social Psychology Bulletin* recounted how they asked half the residents of a large apartment complex to sign a petition favoring the establishment of a recreation center for the handicapped. The cause was good and the request was small, so almost everyone who was asked agreed to sign. Two weeks later, on National Collection Day for the Handicapped, all residents of the complex were approached at home and asked to give to the cause.

A little more than half of those who were not asked to sign the petition made a contribution. But an astounding 92% of those who did sign donated money. The residents of the apartment complex felt obligated to live up to their commitments because those commitments were active, public, and voluntary. These three features are worth considering separately.

There's strong empirical evidence to show that a choice made actively—one that's spoken out loud or written down or otherwise made explicit—is considerably more likely to direct someone's future conduct than the same choice left unspoken. Writing in 1996 in the *Personality and Social Psychology Bulletin*, Delia Cioffi and Randy Garner described an experiment in which college students in one group were asked to fill out a printed form saying they wished to volunteer for an AIDS education project in the public schools. Students in another group volunteered for the same project by leaving blank a form stating that they didn't want to participate. A few days later, when the volunteers reported for duty, 74% of those who showed up were students from the group that signaled their commitment by filling out the form.

The implications are clear for a manager who wants to persuade a subordinate to follow some particular course of action: Get it in writing. Let's suppose you want your employee to submit reports in a more timely fashion. Once you believe you've won agreement, ask him to summarize the decision in a memo and send it to you. By doing so, you'll have greatly increased the odds that he'll fulfill the commitment because, as a rule, people live up to what they have written down.

Research into the social dimensions of commitment suggests that written statements become even more powerful when they're made public. In a classic experiment, described in 1955 in the *Journal of Abnormal and Social Psychology*, college students were asked to estimate the length of lines projected on a screen. Some students were asked to write down their choices on a piece of paper, sign it, and hand the paper to the experimenter. Others wrote their choices on an erasable slate, then erased the slate immediately. Still others were instructed to keep their decisions to themselves.

The experimenters then presented all three groups with evidence that their initial choices may have been wrong. Those who had merely kept their decisions in their heads were the most likely to reconsider their original estimates. More loyal to their first guesses were the students in the group that had written them down and immediately erased them. But by a wide margin, the ones most reluctant to shift from their original choices were those who had signed and handed them to the researcher.

This experiment highlights how much most people wish to appear consistent to others. Consider again the matter of the employee who has been submitting late reports. Recognizing the power of this desire, you should, once you've successfully convinced him of the need to be more timely, reinforce the commitment by making sure it gets a public airing. One way to do that would be to send the employee an email that reads, "I think your plan is just what we need. I showed it to Diane in manufacturing and Phil in shipping, and they thought it was right on target, too." Whatever way such commitments are formalized, they should never be like the New Year's resolutions people privately make and then abandon with no one the wiser. They should be publicly made and visibly posted.

More than 300 years ago, Samuel Butler wrote a couplet that explains succinctly why commitments must be voluntary to be lasting and effective: "He that complies against his will/Is of his own opinion still." If an undertaking is forced, coerced, or imposed from the outside, it's not a commitment; it's an unwelcome burden. Think how you would react if your boss pressured you to donate to the campaign of a political candidate. Would that make you more apt to opt for that candidate in the privacy of a voting booth? Not likely. In fact, in their 1981 book *Psychological Reactance* (Academic Press), Sharon S. Brehm and Jack W. Brehm present data that suggest you'd vote the opposite way just to express your resentment of the boss's coercion.

This kind of backlash can occur in the office, too. Let's return again to that tardy employee. If you want to produce an enduring change in his behavior, you should avoid using threats or pressure tactics to gain his compliance. He'd likely view any change in his behavior as the result of intimidation rather than a personal commitment to change. A better approach would be to identify something that the employee genuinely values in the workplace—high-quality workmanship, perhaps, or team spirit—and then describe how timely reports are consistent with those values. That gives the employee reasons for improvement that he can own. And because he owns them, they'll continue to guide his behavior even when you're not watching.

The principle of authority:
People defer to experts.

The application: Expose your expertise;
don't assume it's self-evident.

Two thousand years ago, the Roman poet Virgil offered this simple counsel to those seeking to choose correctly: "Believe an expert." That may or may not be good advice, but as a description of what people actually do, it can't be beaten. For instance, when the news media present an acknowledged expert's views on a topic, the effect on public opinion is dramatic. A single expert-opinion news story in the *New York Times* is associated with a 2% shift in public opinion nationwide, according to a 1993 study described in the *Public Opinion Quarterly*. And researchers writing in the *American Political Science Review* in 1987 found that when the expert's view was aired on national television, public opinion shifted as much as 4%. A cynic might argue that these findings only illustrate the docile submissiveness of the public. But a fairer explanation is that, amid the teeming complexity of contemporary life, a well-selected expert offers a valuable and efficient shortcut to good decisions. Indeed, some questions, be they legal, financial, medical, or technological, require so much specialized knowledge to answer, we have no choice but to rely on experts.

Since there's good reason to defer to experts, executives should take pains to ensure that they establish their own expertise before they attempt to exert influence. Surprisingly often, people mistakenly assume that others recognize and appreciate their experience. That's what happened at a hospital where some colleagues and I were consulting. The physical therapy staffers were frustrated because so many of their stroke patients abandoned their exercise routines as soon as they left the hospital. No matter how often the staff emphasized the importance of regular home exercise—it is, in fact, crucial to the process of regaining independent function—the message just didn't sink in.

Interviews with some of the patients helped us pinpoint the problem. They were familiar with the background and training of their physicians, but the patients knew little about the credentials of the physical therapists who were urging them to exercise. It was a simple matter to remedy that lack of information: We merely asked the therapy director to display all the awards, diplomas, and certifications of her staff on the walls of the therapy rooms. The result was startling: Exercise compliance jumped 34% and has never dropped since.

What we found immensely gratifying was not just how much we increased compliance, but how. We didn't fool or browbeat any of the patients. We *informed* them into compliance. Nothing had to be invented; no time or resources had to be spent in the process. The staff's expertise was real—all we had to do was make it more visible.

The task for managers who want to establish their claims to expertise is somewhat more difficult. They can't simply nail their diplomas to the wall and wait for everyone to notice. A little subtlety is called for. Outside the United States, it is customary for people to spend time interacting socially before getting down to business for the first time. Frequently they gather for dinner the night before their meeting or negotiation. These get-togethers can make discussions easier and help blunt disagreements—remember the findings about liking and similarity—and they can also provide an opportunity to establish expertise. Perhaps it's a matter of telling an anecdote about successfully solving a problem similar to the one that's on the agenda at the next day's meeting. Or perhaps dinner is the time to describe years spent mastering a complex discipline—not in a boastful way but as part of the ordinary give-and-take of conversation.

Granted, there's not always time for lengthy introductory sessions. But even in the course of the

PERSUASION EXPERTS, SAFE AT LAST

Thanks to several decades of rigorous empirical research by behavioral scientists, our understanding of the how and why of persuasion has never been broader, deeper, or more detailed. But these scientists aren't the first students of the subject. The history of persuasion studies is an ancient and honorable one, and it has generated a long roster of heroes and martyrs.

A renowned student of social influence, William McGuire, contends in a chapter of the *Handbook of Social Psychology*, 3rd edition (Oxford University Press, 1985), that scattered among the more than four millennia of recorded Western history are four centuries in which the study of persuasion flourished as a craft. The first was the Periclean Age of ancient Athens, the second occurred during the years of the

(Continued)

35

PERSUASION EXPERTS, SAFE AT LAST

Roman Republic, the next appeared in the time of the European Renaissance, and the last extended over the hundred years that have just ended, which witnessed the advent of large-scale advertising, information, and mass media campaigns. Each of the three previous centuries of systematic persuasion study was marked by a flowering of human achievement that was suddenly cut short when political authorities had the masters of persuasion killed. The philosopher Socrates is probably the best known of the persuasion experts to run afoul of the powers that be.

Information about the persuasion process is a threat because it creates a base of power entirely separate from the one controlled by political authorities. Faced with a rival source of influence, rulers in previous centuries had few qualms about eliminating those rare individuals who truly understood how to marshal forces that heads of state have never been able to monopolize, such as cleverly crafted language, strategically placed information, and, most important, psychological insight.

It would perhaps be expressing too much faith in human nature to claim that persuasion experts no longer face a threat from those who wield political power. But because the truth about persuasion is no longer the sole possession of a few brilliant, inspired individuals, experts in the field can presumably breathe a little easier. Indeed, since most people in power are interested in remaining in power, they're likely to be more interested in acquiring persuasion skills than abolishing them.

preliminary conversation that precedes most meetings, there is almost always an opportunity to touch lightly on your relevant background and experience as a natural part of a sociable exchange. This initial disclosure of personal information gives you a chance to establish expertise early in the game, so that when the discussion turns to the business at hand, what you have to say will be accorded the respect it deserves.

The principle of scarcity: People want more of what they can have less of.

The application: Highlight unique benefits and exclusive information.

Study after study shows that items and opportunities are seen to be more valuable as they become less available. That's a tremendously useful piece of information for managers. They can harness the scarcity principle with the organizational equivalents of limited-time, limited-supply, and one-of-a-kind offers. Honestly informing a coworker of a closing window of opportunity—the chance to get the boss's ear before she leaves for an extended vacation, perhaps—can mobilize action dramatically.

Managers can learn from retailers how to frame their offers not in terms of what people stand to gain but in terms of what they stand to lose if they don't act on the information. The power of "loss language" was demonstrated in a 1988 study of California homeowners written up in the *Journal of Applied Psychology*. Half were told that if they fully insulated their homes, they would save a certain amount of money each day. The other half were told that if they failed to insulate, they would lose that amount each day. Significantly more people insulated their homes when exposed to the loss language. The same phenomenon occurs in business. According to a 1994 study in the journal *Organizational Behavior and Human Decision Processes*, potential losses figure far more heavily in managers' decision making than potential gains.

In framing their offers, executives should also remember that exclusive information is more persuasive than widely available data. A doctoral student of mine, Amram Knishinsky, wrote his 1982 dissertation on the purchase decisions of wholesale beef buyers. He observed that they more than doubled their orders when they were told that, because of certain weather conditions overseas, there was likely to be a scarcity of foreign beef in the near future. But their orders increased 600% when they were informed that no one else had that information yet.

The persuasive power of exclusivity can be harnessed by any manager who comes into possession of information that's not broadly available and that supports an idea or initiative he or she would like the organization to adopt. The next time that kind of information crosses your desk, round up your organization's key players. The information itself may seem dull, but exclusivity will give it a special sheen. Push it across your desk and say, "I just got this report today. It won't be distributed until next week, but I want to give you an early look at what it shows." Then watch your listeners lean forward.

Allow me to stress here a point that should be obvious. No offer of exclusive information, no exhortation to act now or miss this opportunity forever should be made unless it is genuine. Deceiving colleagues into compliance is not only ethically objectionable, it's foolhardy. If the deception is detected—and it certainly will be—it will snuff out any enthusiasm the offer originally kindled. It will also invite dishonesty toward the deceiver. Remember the rule of reciprocity.

Putting it all together

There's nothing abstruse or obscure about these six principles of persuasion. Indeed, they neatly codify our intuitive understanding of the ways people evaluate information and form decisions. As a result, the principles are easy for most people to grasp, even those with no formal education in psychology. But in the seminars and workshops I conduct, I have learned that two points bear repeated emphasis.

First, although the six principles and their applications can be discussed separately for the sake of clarity, they should be applied in combination to compound their impact. For instance, in discussing the importance of expertise, I suggested that managers use informal, social conversations to establish their credentials. But that conversation affords an opportunity to gain information as well as convey it. While you're showing your dinner companion that you have the skills and experience your business problem demands, you can also learn about your companion's background, likes, and dislikes—information that will help you locate genuine similarities and give sincere compliments. By letting your expertise surface and also establishing rapport, you double your persuasive power. And if you succeed in bringing your dinner partner on board, you may encourage other people to sign on as well, thanks to the persuasive power of social evidence.

The other point I wish to emphasize is that the rules of ethics apply to the science of social influence just as they do to any other technology. Not only is it ethically wrong to trick or trap others into assent, it's ill-advised in practical terms. Dishonest or high-pressure tactics work only in the short run, if at all. Their long-term effects are malignant, especially within an organization that can't function properly without a bedrock level of trust and cooperation.

That point is made vividly in the following account, which a department head for a large textile manufacturer related at a training workshop I conducted. She described a vice president in her company who wrung public commitments from department heads in a highly manipulative manner. Instead of giving his subordinates time to talk or think through his proposals carefully, he would approach them individually at the busiest moment of their workday and describe the benefits of his plan in exhaustive, patience-straining detail. Then he would move in for the kill. "It's very important for me to see you as being on my team on this," he would say. "Can I count on your support?" Intimidated, frazzled, eager to chase the man from their offices so they could get back to work, the department heads would invariably go along with his request. But because the commitments never felt voluntary, the department heads never followed through, and as a result the vice president's initiatives all blew up or petered out.

This story had a deep impact on the other participants in the workshop. Some gulped in shock as they recognized their own manipulative behavior. But what stopped everyone cold was the expression on the department head's face as she recounted the damaging collapse of her superior's proposals. She was smiling.

Nothing I could say would more effectively make the point that the deceptive or coercive use of the principles of social influence is ethically wrong and pragmatically wrongheaded. Yet the same principles, if applied appropriately, can steer decisions correctly. Legitimate expertise, genuine obligations, authentic similarities, real social proof, exclusive news, and freely made commitments can produce choices that are likely to benefit both parties. And any approach that works to everyone's mutual benefit is good business, don't you think? Of course, I don't want to press you into it, but, if you agree, I would love it if you could just jot me a memo to that effect.

ROBERT CIALDINI is the author of *Influence and Pre-Suasion: A Revolutionary Way to Influence and Persuade* (Simon & Schuster, 2016). He is Regents' Professor Emeritus of Psychology and Marketing at Arizona State University and president and CEO of INFLUENCE AT WORK, a global training and keynote company.

Reprinted from *Harvard Business Review*,
October 2001 (product #R0109D).

3

Three Things Managers Should Be Doing Every Day

By Linda A. Hill and Kent Lineback

When are we supposed to do all *that*?" That's the question we constantly get from new managers, only weeks or months into their positions, when we describe the three key activities they should be focusing on to be successful as leaders: building trust, building a team, and building a broader network. To their dismay, most of them have found they rarely end a day in their new positions having done what they planned to do. They spend most of their time solving unexpected problems and making sure their groups do their work on time, on budget, and up to standard. They feel desperately out of control because what's *urgent*—the daily work—always seems to highjack what's *important*—their ongoing work as managers and leaders.

So they push back because they think we've just made their to-do list even longer. And these key elements (we call them the "Three Imperatives of Leading and Managing") are not quick and easy wins—they are substantial and fundamental to one's ability to function effectively as a leader. Here's why:

- *Building trust.* Successful leadership is, at root, about influencing others, and trust is the foundation of all ability to influence others. You cannot influence anyone who does not trust you. Thus the manager must work to cultivate the trust of everyone they work with. They do this by demonstrating the two basic components of trust: competence and character. Competence doesn't mean being the resident expert in everything the group does; it does mean understanding the work well enough to make solid decisions about it and having the courage to ask

questions where they may be less knowledgeable. Character means basing decisions and actions on values that go beyond self-interest and
truly caring about the work, about the customers (internal or external) for whom they do the
work, and about the people doing the work. If
people believe in your competence and character, they will trust you to do the right thing.

- *Building a real team and managing through
  it.* An effective team is bound together by a
  common, compelling purpose, based on shared
  values. In a genuine team, the bonds among
  members are so strong that they truly believe
  they will all succeed or fail together and that
  no individual can win if the team loses. Be-
  sides purpose and values, strong teams also
  have rules of engagement: explicit and im-
  plicit understandings of how members work
  together. For example, what kinds of conflict
  are allowed, and what kinds are not? Smart

leaders make sure all the elements that create a
real team are in place—purpose, values, rules—
and then manage *through* the team. So instead
of saying, "Do it because I'm the boss," they
say, "Do it for the team," which is a much more
powerful approach. In a real team, members
value their membership and strive mightily not
to let their comrades down. The smart leader
builds and uses these powerful ties to shape
behavior.

- *Building a network.* Every team depends on
the support and collaboration of outside people
and groups. Effective group leaders proactively
build and maintain a network of these outsiders, which includes not just those needed for
today's work but also those the group will need
to achieve future goals. This is without a doubt
the imperative that most troubles new managers. They think "networking" is manipulative

organizational politicking that requires them to pretend they like people just because they want something from them. They strive to be above that sort of thing. Alas, in the process, they unnecessarily limit their own and their group's ability to influence others for good ends. Building a network can be politicking, but it need not be if they do it honestly, openly, and with the genuine intent of creating relationships that benefit both sides.

It is here, after covering these imperatives, that we hear the question, "When are we supposed to build trust, build a team, and create a network? How do we do that on top of everything else we have to do?"

Our answer is that the "Three Imperatives" and all that each embodies are not discrete tasks to put on a to-do. Instead, strong, effective leaders manage and lead *through* the daily work. They do this in the way they define, assign, structure, talk about, review, and generally guide that work. They are masters at using the daily work and its inevitable crises to perform their work as managers and leaders.

How do they do this?

They build *trust* by taking the opportunity to demonstrate their ability as they do their daily work, by asking knowledgeable questions and offering insightful suggestions. They use daily decisions and choices to illustrate their own values, expressing their concern for those who work for them or those for whom the group does its work. They reveal themselves, but not in an egotistical way, showing what they know, what they believe, and what they value—and in doing this, they show themselves to be trustworthy.

They build a *team* by using problems and crises in the daily work to remind members of the team's purpose and what it values most. They explain their decisions in these terms. They immediately call out team members who violate a rule of engagement—treating each other disrespectfully, for example—or who place their interests above those of the team. And since the rules apply to all members, including the leader, they ask team members to hold the leader accountable if she ever forgets one of those rules.

They build a *network* by taking opportunities afforded by routine activities—a regular meeting of department heads, for example, or even a chance meeting in the elevator—to build and maintain relationships with colleagues outside their group. They consciously approach problems that involve another group leader in a way that both solves the problem and fosters a long-term relationship. They proactively share information with outsiders who would benefit from it. They encourage their group members to take the same approach when they deal with outsiders.

These are obviously only a few of the ways good managers use their daily work to fulfill the deeper imperatives of leadership, but you get the idea. In fact, if there's anything that might be called a "secret" for not getting overwhelmed by the challenges of becoming an effective manager, this is surely it. We've seen new managers light up when they finally grasp this principle: that the daily work isn't an impediment to doing what good leaders do. Instead, it's *the way*, the vehicle, to do most of what good managers do.

Once they learn this lesson, they look at their daily work differently. For every new task, for every unexpected problem, they take a moment to step back and ask, How can I use this to foster trust? To build and strengthen us as a team? To expand our network and make it stronger?

LINDA A. HILL is the Wallace Brett Donham Professor of Business Administration at Harvard Business School. She is the author of *Becoming a Manager* and a coauthor of *Being the Boss* and *Collective Genius: The Art and Practice of Leading Innovation* (Harvard Business Review Press, 2014). KENT LINEBACK spent many years as a manager and an executive in business and government. He is a coauthor of *Collective Genius: The Art and Practice of Leading Innovation* (Harvard Business Review Press, 2014).

Reprinted from hbr.org, originally published
September 24, 2015 (product #H02DCU).

4

Learning
Charisma

By John Antonakis, Marika Fenley, and Sue Liechti

J ana stands at the podium, palms sweaty, looking out at hundreds of colleagues who are waiting to hear about her new initiative. Bill walks into a meeting after a failed product launch to greet an exhausted and demotivated team that desperately needs his direction. Robin gets ready to confront a brilliant but underperforming subordinate who needs to be put back on track.

We've all been in situations like these. What they require is charisma—the ability to communicate a clear, visionary, and inspirational message that captivates and motivates an audience. So how do you learn charisma? Many people believe that it's impossible.

They say that charismatic people are born that way—as naturally expressive and persuasive extroverts. After all, you can't teach someone to be Winston Churchill.

While we agree with the latter contention, we disagree with the former. Charisma is not all innate; it's a learnable skill or, rather, a set of skills that have been practiced since antiquity. Our research with managers in the laboratory and in the field indicates that anyone trained in what we call "charismatic leadership tactics" (CLTs) can become more influential, trustworthy, and "leader like" in the eyes of others. In this article we'll explain these tactics and how we help managers master them. Just as athletes rely on hard training and the right game plan to win a competition, leaders who want to become charismatic must study the CLTs, practice them religiously, and have a good deployment strategy.

What is charisma?

Charisma is rooted in values and feelings. It's influence born of the alchemy that Aristotle called the *logos*, the *ethos*, and the *pathos*; that is, to persuade others, you must use powerful and reasoned rhetoric, establish personal and moral credibility, and then rouse followers' emotions and passions. If a leader can do those three things well, he or she can then tap into the hopes and ideals of followers, give them a sense of purpose, and inspire them to achieve great things.

Several large-scale studies have shown that charisma can be an invaluable asset in any work context—small or large, public or private, Western or Asian. Politicians know that it's important. Yet many business managers don't use charisma, perhaps because they don't know how to or because they believe it's not as easy to master as transactional (carrot-and-stick) or instrumental (task-based) leadership. Let's be clear: Leaders need technical expertise to win the trust of followers, manage operations, and set strategy; they also benefit from the ability to punish and reward. But the most effective leaders layer charismatic leadership on top of transactional and instrumental leadership to achieve their goals.

In our research, we have identified a dozen key CLTs. Some of them you may recognize as long-standing techniques of oratory. Nine of them are verbal: metaphors, similes, and analogies; stories and anecdotes; contrasts; rhetorical questions; three-part lists; expressions of moral conviction; reflections of the group's sentiments; the setting of high goals; and conveying confidence that they can be achieved. Three tactics are nonverbal: animated voice, facial expressions, and gestures.

There are other CLTs that leaders can use—such as creating a sense of urgency, invoking history, using repetition, talking about sacrifice, and using humor—but the 12 described in this article are the ones that have the greatest effect and can work in almost any context. In studies and experiments, we have found that people who use them appropriately can unite followers around a vision in a way that others can't. In 8 of the past 10 U.S. presidential races, for instance, the candidate who deployed verbal CLTs more often won. And when we measured "good" presentation skills—such as speech structure, clear pronunciation, use of easy-to-understand language, tempo of speech, and speaker comfort—and compared their impact against that of the CLTs, we found that the CLTs played a much bigger role in determining who was perceived to be more leader like, competent, and trustworthy.

Still, these tactics don't seem to be widely known or taught in the business world. The managers who practice them typically learned them by trial and error, without thinking consciously about them. As one manager who attended our training remarked, "I use a lot of these tactics, some without even knowing it." Such learning should not be left to chance.

We teach managers the CLTs by outlining the concepts and then showing news and film clips that highlight examples from business, sports, and politics. Managers must then experiment with and practice the tactics—on video, in front of peers, and on their own. A group of midlevel European executives (with an average age of 35) that did so as part of our training almost doubled their use of CLTs in presentations. As a result, they saw observers' numerical ratings of their competence as leaders jump by about 60% on average. They were then able to take the tactics back to their jobs. We saw the same thing happen with another group of executives (with an average age of 42) in a large Swiss firm. Overall, we've found that about 65% of people who have been trained in the CLTs receive above-average ratings as leaders, in contrast with only 35% of those who have not been trained.

The aim is to use the CLTs not only in public speaking but also in everyday conversations—to be more charismatic all the time. The tactics work because they help you create an emotional connection with followers, even as they make you appear more powerful, competent, and worthy of respect. In Greek, the word "charisma" means special gift. Start to use the CLTs correctly, and that's what people will begin to think you have.

Let's now look at the tactics in detail.

Connect, compare, and contrast

Charismatic speakers help listeners understand, relate to, and remember a message. A powerful way to do this is by using *metaphors*, *similes*, and *analogies*. Martin Luther King Jr. was a master of the metaphor. In his "I Have a Dream" speech, for example, he likened the U.S. Constitution to "a promissory note" guaranteeing the unalienable rights of life, liberty, and the pursuit of happiness to all people but noted that America had instead given its black citizens "a bad check," one that had come back marked "insufficient funds." Everyone knows what it means to receive a bad check. The message is crystal clear and easy to retain.

Metaphors can be effective in any professional context, too. Joe, a manager we worked with, used one to predispose his team to get behind an urgent relocation. He introduced it by saying, "When I heard about this from the board, it was like hearing about a long-awaited pregnancy. The difference is that we have four months instead of nine months to prepare." The team instantly understood it was about to experience an uncomfortable but ultimately rewarding transition.

Stories and anecdotes also make messages more engaging and help listeners connect with the speaker. Even people who aren't born raconteurs can employ them in a compelling way. Take this example from a speech Bill Gates gave at Harvard, urging graduates to consider their broader responsibilities: "My mother . . . never stopped pressing me to do more for others. A few days before my wedding, she hosted a bridal event, at which she read aloud a letter about marriage that she had written to Melinda. My mother was very ill with cancer at the time, but she saw one more opportunity to deliver her message, and at the close of the letter she [quoted]: 'From those to whom much is given, much is expected.'"

Lynn, another manager we studied, used the following story to motivate her reports during a crisis: "This reminds me of the challenge my team and I faced when climbing the Eiger peak a few years ago. We got caught in bad weather, and we could have died up there. But working together, we managed to survive. And we made what at first seemed impossible, possible. Today we are in an economic storm, but by pulling together, we can turn this situation around and succeed." The story made her team feel reassured and inspired.

Contrasts are a key CLT because they combine reason and passion; they clarify your position by pitting it against the opposite, often to dramatic effect. Think of John F. Kennedy's "Ask not what your country can do for you—ask what you can do for your country." In our experience, contrasts are one of the easiest tactics to learn and use, and yet they aren't used enough. Here are some examples from managers newly trained in the CLTs. Gilles, a senior VP, speaking to a direct report managing a stagnant team: "It seems to me that you're playing too much defense when you need to be playing more offense." (That's also a metaphor.) And Sally, introducing herself to her new team: "I asked to lead the medical division not because it has the best location but because I believe we can accomplish something great for our company and at the same time help save lives."

Engage and distill

Rhetorical questions might seem hackneyed, but charismatic leaders use them all the time to encourage engagement. Questions can have an obvious answer or pose a puzzle to be answered later. Think again of Martin Luther King Jr., who said, "There are those who are asking the devotees of civil rights, 'When will you be satisfied?'" and then went on to show that oppressed people can never be satisfied. Anita Roddick—founder of the Body Shop—once used three rhetorical questions to explain what led her to help start the social responsibility movement. The thinking, she said, "was really simple: How do you make business kinder? How do you embed it in the community? How do you make community a social purpose for business?"

This tactic works just as well in private conversations. Take Mika, a manager in our study, who effectively motivated an underperforming subordinate by asking, "So, where do you want to go from here? Will it be back to your office feeling sorry for yourself? Or do you want to show what you are capable of achieving?" Here's another question (also employing metaphor) used by Frank, an IT executive who needed to push back at the unrealistic goals being set for him: "How can you expect me to change an engine in a plane midflight?"

Three-part lists are another old trick of effective persuasion because they distill any message into key takeaways. Why three? Because most people can remember three things, three is sufficient to provide proof of a pattern, and three gives an impression of completeness. Three-part lists can be announced—as in "There are three things we need to do to get our bottom line back into the black"—or they can be under the radar, as in the sentence before this one.

Here's a list that Serge, a midlevel manager, used at a team meeting: "We have the best product on the market. We have the best team. Yet we did not make the sales target." And here's one that Karin, division head of a manufacturing company, employed in a speech to her staff: "We can turn this around with a three-point strategy: First, we need to look back and see what we did right. Next, we need to see where we went wrong. Then, we need to come up with a plan that will convince the board to give us the resources to get it right the next time."

Show integrity, authority, and passion

Expressions of moral conviction and *statements that reflect the sentiments of the group*—even when the sentiments are negative—establish your credibility by revealing the quality of your character to your listeners and making them identify and align themselves with you. On Victory Day at the end of the Second World War, Winston Churchill brilliantly captured the feelings of the British people and also conveyed a spirit of honor, courage, and compassion. He said: "This is your hour. This is not victory of a party or of any class. It's a victory of the great British nation as a whole. We were the first, in this ancient island, to draw the sword against tyranny. . . . There we stood, alone. The lights went out and the bombs came down. But every man, woman, and child in the country had no thought of quitting the struggle. . . . Now we have emerged from one deadly struggle—a terrible foe has been cast on the ground and awaits our judgment and our mercy."

Another nice example of moral conviction (plus a number of other CLTs) comes from Tina, a manager in an NGO pushing for a needed supply-chain change: "Who do you think will pay for the logistical mess we've created? It is not our donors who'll feel it but the children we're supposed to be feeding that will go to bed one more time with an empty belly and who may not make it through the night. Apart from wasting money, this is not right, especially because the fix is so simple." And here's Rami, a senior IT director trained in the CLTs, expertly reflecting the sentiments of his disheartened team: "I know what is going through your minds, because the same thing is going through mine. We all feel disappointed and demotivated. Some of you have told me you have had sleepless nights; others, that there are tensions in the team, even at home because of this. Personally, life to me has become dull and tasteless. I know how hard we have all worked and the bitterness we feel because success just slipped out of our reach. But it's not going to be like this for much longer. I have a plan."

Another CLT, which helps charismatic leaders demonstrate passion—and inspire it in their followers—is *setting high goals*. Gandhi set the almost impossible (and moral) goal of liberating India from British rule without using violence, as laid out in his famous "quit India" speech. An example from the business world that we often cite is the former CEO of Sharp, Katsuhiko Machida. In 1998, at a time when Sharp faced collapse, cathode-ray tubes dominated the TV market, and the idea of using LCD technology was commercially unviable, he energized his employees by stating the unthinkable: "By 2005, all TVs we sell in Japan will be LCD models."

But one must also *convey confidence that the goals can be achieved*. Gandhi noted: "I know the British Government will not be able to withhold freedom from us, when we have made enough self-sacrifice." In a later speech he expressed his conviction more forcefully: "Even if all the United Nations opposes me, even if the whole of India forsakes me, I will say, 'You are wrong. India will wrench with nonviolence her liberty from unwilling hands.' I will go ahead not for India's sake alone but for the sake of the world. Even if my eyes close before there is freedom, nonviolence will not end." Machida personally took his vision to Sharp's engineers to convince them that they could realize his risky goal. He made it the company's most important project, brought together cross-functional teams from LCD and TV development to work on it, and told them plainly that it was crucial to Sharp's survival. Or take Ray, an engineer we know, addressing his team after a setback: "The deadline the CEO gave us is daunting. Other teams would be right to tremble at the knees, but we are not just another team. I know you can rise to the challenge. I believe in each one of you, which means that I believe that we can get the prototype to manufacturing in three months. Let's commit to do what it takes to get the job done: We have the smarts. We have the experience. All we need is the will, and that's something only great teams have." Passion cannot emerge unless the leader truly believes that the vision and strategic goal can be reached.

The three nonverbal cues—*expressions of voice, body, and face*—are also key to charisma. They don't come naturally to everyone, however, and they are the most culturally sensitive tactics: What's perceived as too much passion in certain Asian contexts might be perceived as too muted in southern European ones. But they are nonetheless important to learn and practice because they are easier for your followers to process than the verbal CLTs, and they help you hold people's attention by punctuating your speech. (For more on these, see the sidebar "Charisma in Voice and Body.")

Putting it all into practice

Now that you've learned the CLTs, how do you start using them? Simple: preparation and practice. When you're mapping out a speech or a presentation, you should certainly plan to incorporate the tactics and rehearse them. We also encourage leaders to think about them before one-on-one conversations or team meetings in which they need to be persuasive. The idea is to arm yourself with a few key CLTs that feel comfortable to you and therefore will come out spontaneously—or at least look as if they did. The leaders we've trained worked on improving their charisma in groups and got feedback from one another. You could ask your spouse or a friendly colleague to do the same or videotape yourself and do a self-critique.

The goal isn't to employ all the tactics in every conversation but to use a balanced combination. With time and practice, they will start to come out on the fly. One manager we know, who met his wife after being trained in the CLTs, showed her his "before" videos and told us she couldn't believe it was him. The charismatic guy in the "after" videos—the one whose CLT use had more than doubled—was the person she had married. Another manager, who learned the tactics six years ago and has since become the chief operating officer of his company, says he now uses them every day—personally and professionally—such as in a recent talk to his team about a relocation, which went "much better than expected" as a result.

CHARISMA IN VOICE AND BODY

Three tactics for showing passion—and winning over listeners.

Animated voice

People who are passionate vary the volume with which they speak, whispering at appropriate points or rising to a crescendo to hammer home a point. Emotion—sadness, happiness, excitement, surprise—must come through in the voice. Pauses are also important because they convey control.

Facial expressions

These help reinforce your message. Listeners need to see as well as hear your passion—especially when you're telling a story or reflecting their sentiments. So be sure to make eye contact (one of the givens of charisma), and get comfortable smiling, frowning, and laughing at work.

Gestures

These are signals for your listeners. A fist can reinforce confidence, power, and certitude. Waving a hand, pointing, or pounding a desk can help draw attention.

If you think you can't improve because you're just not naturally charismatic, you're wrong. The managers with the lowest initial charisma ratings in our studies were able to significantly narrow the gap between themselves and their peers to whom the tactics came naturally. It's true that no amount of training or practice will turn you into Churchill or Martin Luther King Jr. But the CLTs can make you more charismatic in the eyes of your followers, and that will invariably make you a more effective leader.

JOHN ANTONAKIS is a professor of business and economics at the University of Lausanne in Switzerland and consults for companies on leadership development. MARIKA FENLEY has a PhD in management focusing on gender and leadership from the Faculty of Business and Economics at the University of Lausanne. SUE LIECHTI holds a master's degree in psychology from the University of Lausanne and is an organizational development consultant.

Reprinted from *Harvard Business Review*,
June 2012 (product #R1206K).

5

To Win People Over, Speak to Their Wants and Needs

By Nancy Duarte

P racticing empathy can be difficult, because you have to step outside your comfort zone to understand someone else's point of view. But it's essential to exercising influence.

It's how method actors move us to feel, think, or act differently—they deeply immerse themselves in their characters, trying on new ways of being and behaving. Sometimes their identity experiments are even part of the story line, as in *Being John Malkovich*, *Avatar*, and *Tootsie*.

During *Tootsie*, walking in the shoes of a woman had such a profound impact on Dustin Hoffman that, 30 years later, recalling his decision to make the film brought tears to his eyes in an interview with the American Film Institute.

Before agreeing to work on the movie, Hoffman did some makeup tests to see if he would be believable as a woman. When he discovered that he could pass, but he wouldn't be *beautiful*, he realized he had to do this project. As he explained to his wife: "I think I'm an interesting woman [as Dorothy Michaels]. And I know that if I met myself at a party, I wouldn't talk to that character because she doesn't fulfill physically the demands that we're brought up to think women have to have in order for us to ask them out . . . There's too many interesting women I have not had the experience to know in this life because I've been brainwashed." Empathy made Hoffman's performance—and the film's message—more convincing and powerful.

The same thing happens in business all the time. Whether you're trying to get your team on board with a new way of working, asking investors to fund you, persuading customers to buy your product, or imploring the public to donate to your cause, your success depends on your ability to grasp the wants and needs of the people around you. We've seen this over and over again at my firm as we've created presentations for clients and coached them on effective delivery. If people feel listened to, they become more receptive to your message. And by doing the listening, you become more informed about what they really need—not just what you think they need—which will fuel your relationships with stakeholders over the long run.

How do you build your capacity for empathy? Exercises can help, and they're used in many fields. Secret shoppers pose as retail customers and record their observations. Product developers brainstorm use cases and interview consumers to envision how they'll interact with a product. Negotiators do role-playing to imagine opposing points of view before they get to the table.

Once you've started to develop empathy as a skill, you can make it integral to the work you do. You might try visualizing stakeholders' various perspectives the way Airbnb CEO Brian Chesky and his team did. As described in a *Fast Company* post, they storyboarded the guest, host, and hiring processes—inspired by Disney's filmmaking. They created a list of the key moments in these three experiences and then developed the most important and most emotionally charged ones into fuller narratives. Cofounder Nathan Blecharczyk says they learned a lot: "What the storyboards made clear is that we were missing a big part of the picture. . . . There were a lot of important moments where we weren't doing anything." The storyboards ended up helping the company define its mobile strategy and even inspired new features, which allowed Airbnb to connect with traveling customers wherever the customers were.[1]

It's also essential to listen carefully to your stakeholders and check your understanding of what's being said. Arbitrators do this to get a handle on what both sides need in a dispute, before trying to carve out a solution. Executives who are new to a company often embark on listening tours with employees and customers to get their perspective on issues and opportunities.

That's what Lou Gerstner did in the 1990s, when the board at IBM brought him in to turn around the almost bankrupt company. Gerstner called his listening tour Operation Bear Hug. He gave managers three months to meet with customers and ask about issues they were grappling with and how IBM could help. Managers then had to recap the conversations in memos. Gerstner also called customers on his own every day. And he "bear-hugged" employees by touring IBM's various sites and hosting gatherings to share updates, test ideas, and tackle concerns. He held 90-minute unscripted Q&A sessions with the staff, during which he would talk to 20,000 workers directly.

"I listened, and I tried very hard not to draw conclusions," Gerstner said.

It was an important step in the strategy-making process, one that enabled the executive team to build plans to make IBM relevant and competitive again. But it led to an even larger shift in IBM's culture that transformed the company from an inwardly focused bureaucracy to a market-driven innovator.

Empathize with the people you need to persuade to purchase your product or services or to work hard on your behalf. It gives you better ideas, and it makes you worth listening to. And if your stakeholders can empathize with you in return, you're on your way to building real, lasting relationships with them.

NANCY DUARTE is CEO of Duarte Design and the author of the *HBR Guide to Persuasive Presentations* (Harvard Business Review Press, 2012), as well as two books on the art of presenting, *Slide:ology: The Art and Science of Creating Great Presentations* (O'Reilly Media, 2008) and *Resonate: Present Visual Stories That Transform Audiences* (Wiley, 2010). She is a coauthor with Patti Sanchez of *Illuminate: Ignite Change Through Speeches, Stories, Ceremonies, and Symbols* (Portfolio, 2016).

Note

1. S. Kessler, "How Snow White Helped Airbnb's Mobile Mission," *Fast Company*, November 8, 2012, http://www.fast cocreate.com/1681924/how-snow-white-helped-airbnbs -mobile-mission; N. Blecharczyk, "Visualizing the Customer Experience," Sequoia Capital, https://www.sequoia cap.com/article/visualizing-customer-experience/; A. Carr, "Inside Airbnb's Grand Hotel Plans," *Fast Company*, March 17, 2014, http://www.fastcompany.com/3027107/ punk-meet-rock-airbnb-brian-chesky-chip-conley.

Reprinted from hbr.org, originally published
May 12, 2015 (product #H0228V).

6

Storytelling That Moves People

An interview with Robert McKee by Bronwyn Fryer

Persuasion is the centerpiece of business activity. Customers must be convinced to buy your company's products or services, employees and colleagues to go along with a new strategic plan or reorganization, investors to buy (or not to sell) your stock, and partners to sign the next deal. But despite the critical importance of persuasion, most executives struggle to communicate, let alone inspire. Too often, they get lost in the accoutrements of company-speak: PowerPoint slides, dry memos, and hyperbolic missives from the corporate communications department. Even the most carefully researched and considered efforts are routinely greeted with cynicism, lassitude, or outright dismissal.

Why is persuasion so difficult, and what can you do to set people on fire? In search of answers to those questions, HBR senior editor Bronwyn Fryer paid a visit to Robert McKee, the world's best known and most respected screenwriting lecturer, at his home in Los Angeles. An award-winning writer and director, McKee moved to California after studying for his PhD in cinema arts at the University of Michigan. He then taught at the University of Southern California's School of Cinema and Television before forming his own company, Two Arts, to take his lectures on the art of storytelling worldwide to an audience of writers, directors, producers, actors, and entertainment executives.

McKee's students have written, directed, and produced hundreds of hit films, including *Forrest Gump*, *Erin Brockovich*, *The Color Purple*, *Gandhi*, *Monty Python and the Holy Grail*, *Sleepless in Se-*

attle, *Toy Story*, and *Nixon*. They have won 18 Academy Awards, 109 Emmy Awards, 19 Writers Guild Awards, and 16 Directors Guild of America Awards. Emmy Award winner Brian Cox portrays McKee in the 2002 film *Adaptation*, which follows the life of a screenwriter trying to adapt the book *The Orchid Thief.* McKee also serves as a project consultant to film and television production companies such as Disney, Pixar, and Paramount as well as major corporations (including Microsoft) that regularly send their entire creative staffs to his lectures.

McKee believes that executives can engage listeners on a whole new level if they toss their PowerPoint slides and learn to tell good stories instead. In his best-selling book *Story: Substance, Structure, Style, and the Principles of Screenwriting*, published in 1997 by HarperCollins, McKee argues that stories "fulfill a profound human need to grasp the patterns of living—not merely as an intellectual exercise, but within a very personal, emotional experience."

What follows is an edited and abridged transcript of McKee's conversation with HBR.

Why should a CEO or a manager pay attention to a screenwriter?

A big part of a CEO's job is to motivate people to reach certain goals. To do that, he or she must engage their emotions, and the key to their hearts is story. There are two ways to persuade people. The first is by using conventional rhetoric, which is what most executives are trained in. It's an intellectual process, and in the business world it usually consists of a PowerPoint slide presentation in which you say, "Here is our company's biggest challenge, and here is what we need to do to prosper." And you build your case by giving statistics and facts and quotes from authorities. But there are two problems with rhetoric. First, the people you're talking to have their own set of authorities, statistics, and experiences. While you're trying to persuade them, they are arguing with you in their heads. Second, if you do succeed in persuading them, you've done so only on an intellectual basis. That's not good enough, because people are not inspired to act by reason alone.

The other way to persuade people—and ultimately a much more powerful way—is by uniting an idea with an emotion. The best way to do that is by telling a compelling story. In a story, you not only weave a lot of information into the telling but you also arouse your listener's emotions and energy. Persuading with a story is hard. Any intelligent person can sit down and make lists. It takes rationality but little creativity to design an argument using conventional rhetoric. But it demands vivid insight and storytelling skill to present an idea that packs enough emotional power to be memorable. If you can harness imagination and the principles of a well-told story, then you get people rising to their feet amid thunderous applause instead of yawning and ignoring you.

So, what is a story?

Essentially, a story expresses how and why life changes. It begins with a situation in which life is relatively in balance: You come to work day after day, week after week, and everything's fine. You expect it will go on that way. But then there's an event—in screenwriting, we call it the "inciting incident"—that throws life out of balance. You get a new job, or the boss dies of a heart attack, or a big customer threatens to leave. The story goes on to describe how, in an effort to restore balance, the protagonist's subjective expectations crash into an uncooperative objective reality. A good storyteller describes what it's like to deal with these opposing forces, calling on the protagonist to dig deeper, work with scarce resources, make difficult decisions, take action despite risks, and ultimately discover the truth. All great storytellers since the dawn of time—from the ancient Greeks through Shakespeare and up to the present day— have dealt with this fundamental conflict between subjective expectation and cruel reality.

How would an executive learn to tell stories?

Stories have been implanted in you thousands of times since your mother took you on her knee. You've read good books, seen movies, attended plays. What's more, human beings naturally *want* to work through stories. Cognitive psychologists describe how the human mind, in its attempt to understand and remember, assembles the bits and pieces of experience into a story, beginning with a personal desire, a life objective, and then

99

portraying the struggle against the forces that block that desire. Stories are how we remember; we tend to forget lists and bullet points.

Businesspeople not only have to understand their companies' past, but then they must project the future. And how do you imagine the future? As a story. You create scenarios in your head of possible future events to try to anticipate the life of your company or your own personal life. So, if a businessperson understands that his or her own mind naturally wants to frame experience in a story, the key to moving an audience is not to resist this impulse but to embrace it by telling a good story.

What makes a good story?

You emphatically do not want to tell a beginning-to-end tale describing how results meet expectations. This is boring and banal. Instead, you want to display the struggle between expectation and reality in all its nastiness.

For example, let's imagine the story of a biotech startup we'll call Chemcorp, whose CEO has to persuade some Wall Street bankers to invest in the company. He could tell them that Chemcorp has discovered a chemical compound that prevents heart attacks and offer up a lot of slides showing them the size of the market, the business plan, the organizational chart, and so on. The bankers would nod politely and stifle yawns while thinking of all the other companies better positioned in Chemcorp's market.

Alternatively, the CEO could turn his pitch into a story, beginning with someone close to him— say, his father—who died of a heart attack. So nature itself is the first antagonist that the CEO-as-protagonist must overcome. The story might unfold like this: In his grief, he realizes that if there had been some chemical indication of heart disease, his father's death could have been pre-vented. His company discovers a protein that's present in the blood just before heart attacks and develops an easy-to-administer, low-cost test.

But now it faces a new antagonist: the FDA. The approval process is fraught with risks and dangers. The FDA turns down the first application, but new research reveals that the test performs even better than anyone had expected, so the agency approves a second application. Meanwhile, Chemcorp is running out of money, and a key partner drops out and goes off to start his own company. Now Chem-corp is in a fight-to-the-finish patent race.

This accumulation of antagonists creates great suspense. The protagonist has raised the idea in the bankers' heads that the story might not have a happy ending. By now, he has them on the edge of their seats, and he says, "We won the race, we got the patent, we're poised to go public and save a quarter-million lives a year." And the bankers just throw money at him.

Aren't you really talking about exaggeration and manipulation?

No. Although businesspeople are often suspicious of stories for the reasons you suggest, the fact is that statistics are used to tell lies and damn lies, while accounting reports are often BS in a ball gown—witness Enron and WorldCom.

When people ask me to help them turn their presentations into stories, I begin by asking questions. I kind of psychoanalyze their companies, and amazing dramas pour out. But most companies and executives sweep the dirty laundry, the difficulties, the antagonists, and the struggle under the carpet. They prefer to present a rosy—and boring—picture to the world. But as a storyteller, you want to position the problems in the foreground and then show how you've overcome them. When you tell the story of your struggles against real antagonists, your audience sees you as an exciting, dynamic person. And I know that the storytelling method works, because after I consulted with a dozen corporations whose principals told exciting stories to Wall Street, they all got their money.

What's wrong with painting a positive picture?

It doesn't ring true. You can send out a press release talking about increased sales and a bright future, but your audience knows it's never that easy. They know you're not spotless; they know your competitor doesn't wear a black hat. They know you've slanted your statement to make your company look good. Positive, hypothetical pictures and boilerplate press releases actually work against you because they foment distrust among the people you're trying to convince. I suspect that most CEOs do not believe their own spin doctors— and if they don't believe the hype, why should the public?

The great irony of existence is that what makes life worth living does not come from the rosy side.

We would all rather be lotus-eaters, but life will not allow it. The energy to live comes from the dark side. It comes from everything that makes us suffer. As we struggle against these negative powers, we're forced to live more deeply, more fully.

So acknowledging this dark side makes you more convincing?

Of course. Because you're more truthful. One of the principles of good storytelling is the understanding that we all live in dread. Fear is when you don't know what's going to happen. Dread is when you know what's going to happen and there's nothing you can do to stop it. Death is the great dread; we all live in an ever-shrinking shadow of time, and between now and then all kinds of bad things could happen.

Most of us repress this dread. We get rid of it by inflicting it on other people through sarcasm, cheating, abuse, indifference—cruelties great and small. We all commit those little evils that relieve the pressure and make us feel better. Then we rationalize our bad behavior and convince ourselves we're good people. Institutions do the same thing: They deny the existence of the negative while inflicting their dread on other institutions or their employees.

If you're a realist, you know that this is human nature; in fact, you realize that this behavior is the foundation of all nature. The imperative in nature is to follow the golden rule of survival: Do unto others what they do unto you. In nature, if you offer cooperation and get cooperation back, you get along. But if you offer cooperation and get antagonism back, then you give antagonism in return—in spades.

Ever since human beings sat around the fire in caves, we've told stories to help us deal with the dread of life and the struggle to survive. All great stories illuminate the dark side. I'm not talking about so-called "pure" evil, because there is no such thing. We are all evil and good, and these sides do continual battle. Kenneth Lay says wiping out people's jobs and life savings was unintentional. Hannibal Lecter is witty, charming, and brilliant, and he eats people's livers. Audiences appreciate the truthfulness of a storyteller who acknowledges the dark side of human beings and deals honestly with antagonistic events. The story engenders a positive but realistic energy in the people who hear it.

Does this mean you have to be a pessimist?

It's not a question of whether you're optimistic or pessimistic. It seems to me that the civilized human being is a skeptic—someone who believes nothing at face value. Skepticism is another principle of the storyteller. The skeptic understands the difference between text and subtext and always seeks what's really going on. The skeptic hunts for the truth beneath the surface of life, knowing that the real thoughts and feelings of institutions or individuals are unconscious and unexpressed. The skeptic is always looking behind the mask. Street kids, for example, with their tattoos, piercings, chains, and leather, wear amazing masks, but the skeptic knows the mask is only a persona. Inside anyone working that hard to look fierce is a marshmallow. Genuinely hard people make no effort.

So, a story that embraces darkness produces a positive energy in listeners?

Absolutely. We follow people in whom we believe. The best leaders I've dealt with—producers and directors—have come to terms with dark reality. Instead of communicating via spin doctors, they lead their actors and crews through the antagonism of a world in which the odds of getting the film made, distributed, and sold to millions of moviegoers are a thousand to one. They appreciate that the people who work for them love the work and live for the small triumphs that contribute to the final triumph.

CEOs, likewise, have to sit at the head of the table or in front of the microphone and navigate their companies through the storms of bad economies and tough competition. If you look your audience in the eye, lay out your really scary challenges, and say, "We'll be lucky as hell if we get through this, but here's what I think we should do," they will listen to you.

To get people behind you, you can tell a truthful story. The story of General Electric is wonderful and has nothing to do with Jack Welch's cult of celebrity. If you have a grand view of life, you can see it on all its complex levels and celebrate it in a story. A great CEO is someone who has come to terms with his or her own mortality and, as a result, has compassion for others. This compassion is expressed in stories.

Take the love of work, for example. Years ago, when I was in graduate school, I worked as an insurance fraud investigator. The claimant in one case was an immigrant who'd suffered a terrible head injury on a carmaker's assembly line. He'd been the fastest window assembler on the line and took great pride in his work. When I spoke to him, he was waiting to have a titanium plate inserted into his head.

The man had been grievously injured, but the company thought he was a fraud. In spite of that, he remained incredibly dedicated. All he wanted was to get back to work. He knew the value of work, no matter how repetitive. He took pride in it and even in the company that had falsely accused him. How wonderful it would have been for the CEO of that car company to tell the tale of how his managers recognized the falseness of their accusation and then rewarded the employee for his dedication. The company, in turn, would have been rewarded with redoubled effort from all the employees who heard that story.

How do storytellers discover and unearth the stories that want to be told?

The storyteller discovers a story by asking certain key questions. First, what does my protagonist want in order to restore balance in his or her life? Desire is the blood of a story. Desire is not a shopping list but a core need that, if satisfied, would stop the story in its tracks. Next, what is keeping my protagonist from achieving his or her desire? Forces within? Doubt? Fear? Confusion? Personal conflicts with friends, family, lovers? Social conflicts arising in the various institutions in society? Physical conflicts? The forces of Mother Nature? Lethal diseases in the air? Not enough time to get things done? The damned automobile that won't start? Antagonists come from people, society, time, space, and every object in it, or any combination of these forces at once. Then, how would my protagonist decide to act in order to achieve his or her desire in the face of these antagonistic forces? It's in the answer to that question that storytellers discover the truth of their characters, because the heart of a human being is revealed in the choices he or she makes under pressure. Finally, the storyteller leans back from the design of events he or she has created and asks, "Do I believe this? Is it neither an exaggeration nor a soft-soaping of the struggle? Is this an honest telling, though heaven may fall?"

Does being a good storyteller make you a good leader?

Not necessarily, but if you understand the principles of storytelling, you probably have a good understanding of yourself and of human nature, and that tilts the odds in your favor. I can teach the formal principles of stories, but not to a person who hasn't really lived. The art of storytelling takes intelligence, but it also demands a life experience that I've noted in gifted film directors: the pain of childhood. Childhood trauma forces you into a kind of mild schizophrenia that makes you see life simultaneously in two ways: First, it's direct, real-time experience, but at the same moment, your brain records it as material—material out of which you will create business ideas, science, or art. Like a double-edged knife, the creative mind cuts to the truth of self and the humanity of others.

Self-knowledge is the root of all great storytelling. A storyteller creates all characters from the self by asking the question, "If I were this character in these circumstances, what would I do?" The more you understand your own humanity, the more you can appreciate the humanity of others in all their good-versus-evil struggles. I would argue that the great leaders Jim Collins describes are people with enormous self-knowledge. They have self-insight and self-respect balanced by skepticism. Great storytellers—and, I suspect, great leaders—are skeptics who understand their own masks as well as the masks of life, and this understanding makes them humble. They see the humanity in others and deal with them in a compassionate yet realistic way. That duality makes for a wonderful leader.

ROBERT MCKEE is a celebrated screenwriting instructor formerly at the University of Southern California's School of Cinema and Television. His firm, Two Arts, brings his seminars on the art of storytelling worldwide to a broad audience of screenwriters, novelists, playwrights, poets, documentary makers, producers, and directors. BRONWYN FRYER is a collaborative writer and former senior editor with the *Harvard Business Review*.

Reprinted from *Harvard Business Review*,
June 2003 (product #R0306B).

7

The Surprising Persuasiveness of a Sticky Note

By Kevin Hogan

magine that you really need to convince someone to do something, such as follow through on a task. You might be surprised to learn that one of the best ways to get someone to comply with your request is through a tiny nuance that adds a personal touch: attaching a sticky note.

A brilliant set of experiments by Randy Garner at Sam Houston State University in Huntsville, Texas, found that a) adding a personal touch, and b) making someone feel like you're asking a favor of them (and not just anyone) can bring about impressive results when done in tandem.[1]

The goal of Garner's experiments was to see what was necessary to generate compliance in completing surveys—which are often quite lengthy and tedious—by fellow professors at the university, using only interoffice mail as the conduit of communication. The wild card factor in these experiments was the use of sticky notes. In one experiment, he sent surveys to three separate groups of 50 professors (150 professors total). Three groups received three different requests, as follows:

> *Group 1* received a survey with a sticky note attached asking for the return of the completed survey.

> *Group 2* received a survey with the same handwritten message on the cover letter instead of an attached sticky note.

> *Group 3* received a survey with a cover letter but no handwritten message.

What happened?

> *Group 3*: 36% of the professors returned the survey.

> *Group 2*: 48% of the professors returned the survey.

> *Group 1*: 76% of the professors returned the survey.

Generalizing this experiment in other contexts simply requires understanding *why* the sticky note worked so well. It represents many powerful behavioral triggers all in one little object:

1. It doesn't match the environment: The sticky note takes up space and looks a bit cluttered. The brain, therefore, wants it gone.

2. It gets attention first because of #1. It's difficult to ignore.

3. It's personalized. (That's the difference between Group 2 and Group 3 in the experiment.)

4. Ultimately, the sticky note represents *one person* communicating with *another important person*—almost as if it is a favor or special request, which makes the recipient feel important.

Garner couldn't help but explore the sticky note factor further. He decided to do a second experiment where he sent a group of professors a *blank* sticky note attached to one of the surveys. Here's what happened:

Group 1 received a survey with a personalized sticky note message.

Group 2 received a survey with a blank sticky note attached.

Group 3 received a survey with no sticky note.

What happened in the second study?

Group 3: 34% returned the survey with no sticky note (similar to the first experiment).

Group 2: 43% returned the survey with the blank sticky note

Group 1: 69% returned the survey with the personalized sticky note (similar to the first experiment).

The real magic, it seems, is not the sticky note itself but the sense of connection, meaning, and identity that the sticky note represents. The person sending the survey is *personally* asking *me* in a special way (not just writing it on the survey) to help him or her out.

But there's more to compliance than just the result. There's also the speed of compliance and the quality of the effort. Garner experimented to see how quickly people would return a follow-up survey if there was a sticky note attached and also measured how much information the person being surveyed returned if there was a sticky note attached versus the group that received no sticky note. Here's what he found:

> *Group 1* (with sticky note) returned their self-addressed stamped envelopes (SASEs) and surveys within an average of about 4 days.
>
> *Group 2* (no sticky note) returned their SASEs and surveys in an average of about 5 1/2 days.

But the most notable difference is that Group 1 also sent significantly more comments and answered other open-ended questions with more words than Group 2 did.

Further experiments revealed that if a task is easy to perform or comply with, a simple sticky note request needs no further personalization. But when the task is more involved, a more highly personalized sticky note was significantly more effective than a simple standard sticky note request. What makes it truly personal? Writing a brief message is effective, but adding the person's first name at the top and your initials at the bottom causes significantly greater compliance.

I've used this personalization theory with businesspeople around the world to great success. For example, a mortgage broker I worked with tested this approach in mailings, effectively doubling the number of phone calls from people pursuing a loan with the broker. And it's not just effective at the office or with clients. The people you live with are going to respond to the sticky note model as well. (Try sticking one on the bathroom mirror and see what happens.)

Recently, the personalized sticky note has been put into digital form for use in email, with mixed results. It's most effective in email when the two people have met or know each other. It had only a modest effect in sales letters designed to make an immediate sale, when the reader didn't know the author of the sales letter. Using the notes in sales letters designed for current clients and customers needs further testing.

The next time you need colleagues to comply with a request, or the next time you're giving a potential client a portfolio to review, try leaving a sticky note. A small personal touch will go a long way toward getting the results you want.

KEVIN HOGAN is the author of 21 books, including *The Science of Influence: How to Get Anyone to Say Yes* (Wiley, 2010) and *The Psychology of Persuasion: How to Persuade Others to Your Way of Thinking* (Pelican Publishing, 1996).

Note

1. R. Garner, "Post-it Note Persuasion: A Sticky Influence," and "What's In a Name? Persuasion Perhaps," *Journal of Consumer Psychology*, 2005.

Reprinted from hbr.org, originally published May 26, 2015 (product #H023LE).

8

When to Sell with Facts and Figures, and When to Appeal to Emotions

By Michael D. Harris

When should salespeople sell with facts and figures, and when should they try to speak to the buyer's emotional subconscious instead? When do you talk to Mr. Intuitive and when to Mr. Rational?

I'd argue that too often, selling to Mr. Rational leads to analysis paralysis, especially for complex products or services. And yet many of us continue to market almost exclusively to Mr. Rational. The result is that we spend too much time chasing sales opportunities that eventually stall out. We need to improve our ability to sell to Mr. Intuitive.

We default to selling to Mr. Rational because when we think of ourselves, we identify with our conscious rational mind. We can't imagine that serious executives would make decisions based on emotion, because we view our emotional decisions as irrational and irresponsible.

But what if Mr. Intuitive has a logic of his own? In recent years, psychologists and behavioral economists have shown that our emotional decisions are neither irrational nor irresponsible. In fact, we now understand that our unconscious decisions do in fact follow a clear logic. They are based on a deeply empirical mental-processing system that is capable of effortlessly cycling through millions of bits of data without getting overwhelmed. Our conscious mind, on the other hand, has a strict bottleneck, because it can only process three or four new pieces of information at a time due to the limitations of our working memory.[1]

The Iowa Gambling Task study, for example, highlights how effective the emotional brain is at effortlessly figuring out the probability of success for maximum gain.[2] Subjects were given an imaginary budget and four stacks of cards. The objective of the game was to win as much money as possible, and to do so, subjects were instructed to draw cards from any of the four decks.

The subjects were not aware that the decks were carefully prepared. Drawing from two of the decks led to consistent wins, while the other two had high payouts but carried oversized punishments. The logical choice was to avoid the dangerous decks, and after about 50 cards, people did stop drawing from the risky decks. It wasn't until the 80th card, however, that people could explain why. Logic is slow.

But the researchers tracked the subjects' anxiety and found that people started to become nervous when reaching for the risky deck after drawing only 10 cards. Intuition is fast.

Harvard Business School professor Gerald Zaltman says that 95% of our purchase decisions take place unconsciously. But why, then, are we not able to look back through our decision history and find countless examples of emotional decisions? Because our conscious mind will always make up reasons to justify our unconscious decisions.

In a study of people who'd had the left and right hemisphere of their brains severed in order to prevent future epileptic seizures, scientists were able to deliver a message to the right side of the brain to "Go to the water fountain down the hall and get a drink."[3] After seeing the message, the subject would get up and start to leave the room, and that's when the scientist would deliver a message to the opposite, left side of the brain, asking, "Where are you going?" Now remember, the left side of the brain never saw the message about the fountain. But did the left brain admit it didn't know the answer? No. Instead it shamelessly fabricated a rational reason, something like, "It's cold in here. I'm going to get my jacket."

So if you can't reliably use your own decision-making history as a guide, when do you know you should be selling based on logic and when on emotion?

Here's the short rule of thumb: Sell to Mr. Rational for simple sales and to Mr. Intuitive for complex sales.

This conclusion is backed by a 2011 study based on subjects selecting the best used car from a selection of four cars. Each car was rated in four different categories (such as gas mileage). But one car clearly had the best attributes. In this "easy" situation with only four variables, the conscious deciders were 15% better at choosing the best car than the unconscious deciders. When the researchers made the decision more complex—ratcheting the number of variables up to 12—unconscious deciders were 42% better than conscious deciders at selecting the best car. Many other studies have shown how our conscious minds become overloaded by too much information.

If you want to influence how a customer feels about your product, provide an experience that creates the desired emotion. One of the best ways for a customer to experience your complex product is by sharing a vivid customer story. Research has shown that stories can activate the region of the brain that processes sights, sounds, tastes, and movement.[4] Contrast this approach with that of a salesperson delivering a data dump in the form of an 85-slide PowerPoint presentation.

Rather than thinking of the emotional mind as irrational, think of it this way: An emotion is simply the way the unconscious communicates its decision to the conscious mind.

MICHAEL D. HARRIS is the CEO of Insight Demand and the author of *Insight Selling: Surprising Research on What Sales Winners Do Differently* (Wiley, 2014).

Notes

1. N. Cowan, "The Magical Number 4 in Short-Term Memory: A Reconsideration of Mental Storage Capacity," *Behavioral Brain Science* 24, no. 1 (February 2001): 87–114.
2. A. Bechara et al., "Insensitivity to Future Consequences Following Damage to Human Prefrontal Cortex," *Cognition* 50, no. 1–3 (April–June 1995): 7–15.

3. M. S. Gazzaniga, "The Split Brain Revisited," *Scientific American*, July 1, 1998.
4. G. Everding, "Readers Build Vivid Mental Simulations of Narrative Situations, Brain Scans Suggest," Medical Xpress, January 26, 2009, https://medicalxpress .com/news/2009-01-readers-vivid-mental-simulations -narrative.html.

Reprinted from hbr.org, originally published
January 26, 2015 (product #H01U9Y).

Index

How to be human at work.

HBR's Emotional Intelligence Series features smart, essential reading on the human side of professional life from the pages of *Harvard Business Review*. Each book in the series offers uplifting stories, practical advice, and research from leading experts on how to tend to our emotional well-being at work.

Harvard Business Review
Emotional Intelligence Series

Available in paperback or ebook format. The specially priced six-volume set includes:

- Mindfulness
- Resilience
- Influence and Persuasion

- Authentic Leadership
- Happiness
- Empathy